DARING

WITH

RUTH

18 Devotionals to Ignite Your
Courage, Transform Your Hope,
and Reveal God's True Character

David Ramos

Thank You!

I appreciate you taking the time to check out my book. As a thank you, I would like to send you the gift *Dreaming with Joseph: 12 Devotionals to Inspire Your Faith, Encourage Your Heart, and Help Your Realize God's Plan.*

To claim your FREE copy simply go to RamosAuthor.com and enter your email address.

.

Table of Contents

Introduction

I was raised by two strong, Godly women. My grandma was, and is, the closest thing to a living saint I have ever known. From what I hear, she wasn't always this way. But God had a way of bringing her into His plans and she's been a shining example of His provision and patience ever since.

The second woman is my mother. In many ways, she reminds me of Ruth: entirely motivated by the well-being of those closest to her while simultaneously acting out of a headstrong stubbornness. God has used her character, more than a few times, to save me from myself and to get my eyes back on what really matters.

I owe so much of my spiritual maturity to the example of these two women. And in a similar way, I believe many of the great characters we read about in Scripture owe something to Ruth as well.

Ruth is like a silent hurricane of good. Her posture and character cause her, at least initially, to be unassuming. But like a powerful force of nature, once she moves she impacts everything and everyone around her for the better. In four short chapters, she goes from being a foreign widow to becoming the ancestor of Jesus! How is this possible and how can we follow her example?

Ruth's life can be boiled down into three simple words: boldness, surrender, and hope.

What I pray you will gain over the next 18 days is an intimate understanding of how our actions can work alongside God's will. God has not called us to sit on the sidelines while He moves and changes the world. Instead, He has summoned us to be a part of His great work. To be bold. To trust in Him. And to hope – fiercely – even when the whole world around us seems to have given up. Especially then.

While you may be waiting on God to act, He is waiting on you. Don't be satisfied with anything less than a life which is unexplainable apart from God's intervention. I invite you now into this lesson on courage, this story of hope, and this opportunity to become daring with Ruth...

An Unexpected Detour

Day 1

Ruth 1:1-2

The story of Ruth begins with the family she would soon marry into. Elimelek, Naomi, and their two sons flee from their home in Bethlehem because famine has struck the land. For modern readers, we hear the word famine and immediately think of the danger involved. Ancient Israelite readers may have had a different reaction.

Famine prompted Abraham to go to Egypt, and led to Joseph's family being reunited.[i] In the Old Testament, famine was a tool God used to move his people into the path of promise. Though the main characters felt like they were off track, or reacting out of fear – God would show up and redeem the situation in a powerful way.

As we enter the well-known story of Ruth, it's hard not to think about the tragedy that is right around the corner. We know that Elimelek's detour did not lead to a better life for his entire family in the way he had hoped. And the Bible never tells us if he traveled to Moab out of obedience or fear.

What we can know is that the presence of trouble (*like famine*) does not equal the absence of God. In fact, the presence of difficulty is often God laying the foundation for his greater work to come true.

Ruth's story is ultimately one of redemption, where God shows up, takes a girl no one knows, and makes her an essential part of the history of the world. And it all started with a family fleeing a famine.

Don't begrudge the detours life may make you take. God knows exactly what he is doing with every trouble and delay we face.

Takeaway: Sometimes life's detours are God's shortcuts.

Prayer: Thank You Lord that you are guiding my life and my story. Help me to trust You in every difficult season.

Pain And Provision

Day 2
Ruth 1:3-5

The rocky beginning of the book of Ruth takes a very dark turn.

The husband who led his family away from their homeland for protection has passed away. We can only imagine what must have gone through Naomi's mind. Then, a glimmer of hope appeared as both of her sons marry local women. However, the joy was short lived. Naomi and her newly extended family live in the foreign land for ten more years before both of her sons follow their father into the afterlife.

Naomi and her two daughters-in-law are left completely alone. No one to help take care of them. No children to show for their years of marriage.

Readers come to this passage and are shocked by the extremity of their suffering. Why did this have to happen? Was the family being punished for not staying in Bethlehem? Was it wrong for them to stay and settle in secular Moab?

We can offer many different ideas, but it's best to rely most heavily upon the text. The narrator of this story remains silent on so many things. They never tell us what led to Elimelek and his sons' deaths. We don't know why Ruth and Orpah did not bear children. We never even get a glimpse into how God may be working this out for His good.

But what we can see is a pattern beginning to develop.[ii] Commentator Robert Hubbard writes that *"by comparing Naomi to other well-known childless women (Sarah, Rachel, Hannah, etc.), he hints that her fate might also conform to a pattern: if Naomi somehow obtains offspring against such impossible odds, it will only the be the work of God; and a divinely given birth forecasts a heroic destiny for the child."*

The beginning of Ruth's story is a call for us to trust in God's unchanging nature.[iii] At this point in the story, we, as readers, are left all but hopeless. Unless, that is, we turn our eyes from the situation at hand and turn them towards the stories of God's goodness which have carried us to this point. Sarah bore Isaac who became the father of the twelve tribes of Israel. Hannah bore Samuel who became one of Israel's greatest prophets and was nicknamed the *Kingmaker*.

Profound pain, when placed in the hands of God, leads to profound opportunity. But only if we are willing.

Takeaway: Painful periods in life are opportunities to trust in God's pattern of provision.

Prayer: God, I may not understand why this is happening, but I put my trust in you to carry me through it. Nothing is impossible with You.[iv]

David Ramos

Anger Versus Trust

Day 3

Ruth 1: 6-13

The pain of Naomi's situation has become too much to bear. Moab has brought her and her family nothing but trouble; so, she decides to journey back to the land of Judah. She sets off with her two daughters-in-law, but midway into their journey she urges them to turn back.

It's probable Naomi did not change her mind during the trip but planned for it to happen this way. If she confronted them while still in Moab, they might have convinced her to stay. It would be easier for them to go their separate ways while out in the open. On top of this, Naomi is not simply telling them goodbye but releasing them from their familial duty. *May the LORD show you kindness* was a phrase used in Ancient Israel to formally end a relationship.[v] Naomi is set on returning home, and living out the rest of her days alone.

The two daughters offer to go with her. After all, they had bonded over the last decade through a series of extreme circumstances. Those bonds are not easily broken. But Naomi insists. She says God is against her; and from an outside view, it seems like Naomi might be right. In just the first few verses she has faced famine, death, and barrenness. Maybe her troubles will continue?

Hubbard writes something interesting about Naomi's response here. He says, "By holding Yahweh responsible for her losses, Naomi affirmed his participation in the events."[vi] To put it another way, Naomi's complaining about God showed that she still believed he was involved in her life. In some small way, her lament was also a cry for hope; because if God could allow these things to happen, He could also find a way to fix them.

Faith and trust in God does not always look like worship songs and praise reports. Sometimes, honest faith looks like anger. Sometimes, honest trust looks like pain.

Many Christians (me included) have gotten the idea in our heads that if we are not cheery around God, He is going to punish us. When, in fact, that couldn't be further from the truth. He longs for our whole selves. He wants to hear the words we are afraid to say. He can take it.

This intimate look at Naomi reveals to us that it's possible to be disappointed in God and yet still hope in His goodness.

Takeaway: It's possible to be angry at God and still trust in Him.

Prayer: Lord, help me to know that You have my best in mind. Even when everything around me tries to tell me differently. I trust in You.

David Ramos

Unlikely But Willing

Day 4
Ruth 1:14-18

After Naomi's powerful plea for her daughters to return home, the text turns its attention towards Orpah and Ruth.

Orpah obeys her mother-in-law. After taking a moment to weep this loss, Orpah kisses Naomi and ventures back to her homeland and to her people.

Ruth chooses differently. Without a word, at first, Ruth refuses to let go of Naomi. Even more than that, the wording the narrator chooses to use sheds some light about Ruth's disposition. Ruth's "clinging to" is not only her choosing Naomi, but the abandonment of her heritage.[vii]

Naomi tries, once again, to urge her to go back to her homeland where she has at least a chance at a normal life. But Ruth replies with one of the most beautiful sections in the Old Testament:

Your people will be my people and your God my God.

Why would Ruth react like this? She was willing to trade everything she had ever known for what? All she has seen of Naomi's God was that He did not protect her from extreme pain and loss. Unlike Abraham, or other patriarchs, God did not speak to her or promise her any sort of redemption.

I believe at this point we are seeing two things at play: Ruth's noble character and the pull of God's Spirit. Ruth is a rare combination of loyalty, love, and an appetite for risk. From this one scene alone, I wish I could be more like her!

God knew her character and seized the opportunity to make her a part of the greatest story ever told. Here was this Moabite woman, someone who would have been looked at with suspicion and even disgust by many Israelites, yet who portrayed amazing qualities and a willingness to accept Yahweh as Lord.

Ruth was an unlikely hero for so many reasons: her heritage, her beliefs, her circumstances. But she was the perfect candidate for one: she dared to let go and put her life and her future completely in God's hands.

Takeaway: Never underestimate what God can do with a willing soul.

Prayer: Thank you Lord for always being patient with me. Please grow a willingness in my soul that You can use for great things.

David Ramos

A Season's Change

Day 5
Ruth 1:19-22

Together, Ruth and Naomi finally make it to their destination: Bethlehem, Naomi's original homeland.

The scene begins with a glimmer of excitement and hope. The entire town is "stirred" by Naomi's return. But their excitement soon turns into something else. Naomi is different. Never mind the fact that she has arrived alone, except for a mysterious foreign girl. Her demeanor has changed. The once beautiful and lively woman is now cold, distant.

Naomi confirms the change telling her old neighbors and friends to call her Mara, which means *bitter*. In all of Scripture, Naomi is the only person to change her own name. Most often, name changes are instituted by God or a human ruler. Here, Naomi takes it upon herself to redefine her identity.

If you keep reading, you'll discover something interesting. The narrator never uses the name Mara again in the entire book of Ruth. In fact, it appears that everyone continued to call her Naomi.

Name changes were meant to signify a permanent transformation. For example, Jacob, which means *the deceiver*, was changed to Israel, which means *one who triumphs with God*. The new name signified the new chapter in Jacob's life. Naomi believed that God had resigned her to live a bitter life for the rest of her days. But the writer of the text and Naomi's friends all refused to believe that would be her fate. They continued to call her by her real, God-given name which meant *lovely*.

Almost as another argument against Naomi's desire to become Mara, Chapter 1 ends by stating that the harvest season was just getting started. Everything around Naomi, even nature itself, was urging her to look beyond herself and to remember this one truth: seasons change.

Like Naomi, we will be tempted to define ourselves by the season of life we are in. *Bitter, broken, sick, scared.* When you begin to feel this way, stop what you are doing and take a moment to look outside.

Before autumn, the leaves begin to reveal another color. Before winter, those same leaves find their way off their branches and onto the wind. Before spring, the snow begins to melt away. And before summer, small flower buds begin to spring up from where the snow once was.

God has instituted a year-round reminder that life will not always be the way it is right now. When things are good, be grateful because life is short. And when things are bad, be hopeful because in the grand scheme of things, our troubles are even shorter.

Takeaway: Life is a series of seasons. Your current trouble will eventually bloom into something good.

Prayer: You are a good God. Help me believe in your goodness, even when my small view of life only sees trouble.

David Ramos

Miracle In The Works

Day 6

Ruth 2:1

Change, opportunity, divine intervention – these come into our lives in all sorts of ways.

After the scene of Ruth and Naomi's entrance into the city of Bethlehem, we can assume that news spread to everyone about her misfortune, and also about the unique loyalty of the daughter-in-law who followed her home.

Now, as we step into Chapter 2, the writer of Ruth does not want us concerned with everyone in Bethlehem. Instead, we are shown a single character: a man by the name of Boaz.

We learn three things about the man in just the first verse. First, he was a relative of Naomi. Second, he was a relative from the same clan as Naomi's husband. Third, he was a "man of standing" which translated other ways implies that he was wealthy, capable, and possibly a war hero.[viii]

Naomi and Ruth have no idea how this character will soon impact their story; and, at this point, neither do we.

There's a literary device writers use when telling stories called *deus ex machina*. It's a technique where the author of the story inserts something unlikely or even impossible to save the day. For example, a hero finds the only weapon that can kill the monster in front of him. Or a mysterious source comes forward and gives the reporter exactly what she needs to finish the story. When it's done well, it can be incredibly gratifying for the audience. But when it's done poorly, it can feel like a cop-out by the storyteller.

As we will see, Boaz is a sort of *deus ex machina* – an unlikely subject who dramatically changes the direction of the story for the better.

What I want to take a minute to ask is, why don't we ever look for these instances of God's intervention in our own lives? I know personally, I was raised with the idea that God helps those who help themselves. But what if this isn't the entire picture?

As we read through Scripture and watch the patterns of how God interacts with his people, what we see is that *deus ex machina*, or unlikely interventions, are one of God's favorite ways of dramatically changing the lives of his chosen ones. Abraham heard a voice out of nowhere; Jacob wrestled with God; the young boy David had the most renown prophet in Israel tell him he would one day be king, and the disciples had the Son of God personally invite them to help him build a new kingdom.

God loves to do the unlikely and the impossible. He shines brightest when things are at their darkest, because that is when there can be no other explanation but His goodness.

Takeaway: God still works miracles today.

Prayer: Heavenly Father, I believe in your miracles. Remind me today that You are above all things, and that all things must answer to You.

David Ramos

More Than Gleanings

Day 7
Ruth 2:2-7

As soon as Ruth and Naomi arrive at whatever place they will now be calling home, Ruth asks for permission to work. Her drive offers us another look into her character. She did not come all this way with Naomi to just sit and beg. She will do everything she can to care for herself and her mother-in-law.

Now, before we dive into what the text says, we have to do some rearranging first. After digging into a handful of commentaries, it seems that we have been reading verses 2-7 a little out of order. At first, it appears that Ruth immediately finds a field and begins working. That field happens to belong to Boaz who notices the hard-working woman when he arrives back home. But this isn't exactly what happens.

Verse 3, the one which says that Ruth began to

glean, acts more like a summary of what *will* happen, not what *did* happen. If verse 3 is the summary, then verse 4 is where the scene begins. Boaz arrives home, greets his harvesters, and immediately asks who the young woman is. Why would he turn his attention to her so quickly? The answer is simple – she was standing right there.

Why was she just standing there "all morning?" I promise, by diving this deep into the text, you are going to discover more about Ruth than you ever have before.

She was standing there, because she asked for something extraordinary. It was Israelite law that the impoverished could glean in the fields. What that meant is that they would follow behind all of the other workers and pick up what was left behind. Harvesting the crops was a multi-person, multi-group operation. The gleaners were at the very back and would pick up the scraps the harvesters didn't see as valuable enough to pick up.

Ruth didn't want to be at the very back. The original text leads many scholars to believe that she wanted to be somewhere closer to the front where she could pick up incredibly more grain.

Was Ruth greedy? Not in the least. Trying to live off the gleanings back then would have been like trying to live off recycled aluminum cans today. You may be able to buy a meal, but there's no way you could support a loved one and keep a roof over your head.

Ruth was bold, courageous. She asked for the opportunity to provide for herself and her mother-in-law in a significant way and stood there waiting until the man in charge gave her an answer.

This scene is not just about Ruth being a hard-working woman. It's about her patience, her humility, and her persistence. When you think of Ruth, don't have a quiet, reserved woman in your mind. She is a beautiful combination of respect and fearlessness, and we can learn much from her actions.

Over and over again, Scripture encourages us to be bold. To shake off our timidity and to go after the things God has placed in our hearts.[ix] I truly believe people would see more of their prayers answered if they took more courageous actions.

I prayed for a wife for many years. But it wasn't until I actually pursued a beautiful woman that I received an answer to my prayers. When I was in a long season of unemployment, I prayed every day for God to open up the right door. But I also sent out applications, made phone calls, and networked in person until that prayer was answered and I was employed once again.

The most prevalent lesson in the book of Ruth is that God wants our deep prayers to be met with bold action. It is our courage which invites His goodness, our small effort which paves the way for His great movements.

Takeaway: Deep prayers and courageous actions invite God's incredible goodness into our lives.

Prayer: I am powerless on my own Lord. But with You all things are possible. My God is mighty indeed!

A Good God

Day 8
Ruth 2:8-13

Ruth's bold actions are met with a gracious reply from Boaz. He not only grants her the request but urges her to stay. He promises she will be treated not only fairly, but far above what could be expected for someone in her position.

We could imagine the surprise Ruth must have felt. Her risky gamble had paid off. Even if this is what she had hoped for, she is still caught off guard by Boaz's kindness. As he explains, the story of her character preceded her.

Boaz recounts all the sacrifices Ruth made to get to this point and sees his small gesture of kindness as simply the beginning of God repaying her for what she gave up.

What catches my attention most in these few verses is Boaz's view of God. Up until now, Naomi has been the only one describing her Lord. He comes across as fickle, angry, and detached towards her pain. In Boaz's speech, we see something entirely different. Boaz's God is one who repays His debts, who rewards the sacrifices of His children and who, like a caring parent, covers His children under the protection of His wings.

All of us have a view of God colored by our life experiences. For some, a good life has led us to see God as just, present, and powerful. For others, suffering has made us question God's ability to help us, and if He even cares.

Only God can change our view of God. You could read a thousand books about God's grace, but until you experience it in your own life – you will never know the extent to which He can transform you. The same goes for any other of His infinite qualities: justice, kindness, provision, love. It's only when God steps in and invites us to experience the kind of God He really is that our lives and perspectives are changed forever.

Naomi was not a bad person for believing what she did about God. She was simply in the process of being brought to a place where God could change her mind.

If you are in a season of believing like Naomi – that

God is too far and cares too little to give you what you need – all I can say is be patient. God is good. I can say that wholeheartedly, not because of the books I have read, or even the ones I have written, but because of the experiences of His character in my own life.

Takeaway: God cares more than you could fathom and is closer than you think.

Prayer: Thank You God for being the type of caregiver we could never deserve, but the One we deeply need.

David Ramos

Unlocking God's Provision

Day 9
Ruth 2:14-17

As we continue into the scene with Boaz and Ruth, we see him doing everything he can to care for this young stranger.

Boaz invites Ruth to eat at his table with his workers: a clear gesture that he respected her company. Next, as she goes out to work, Boaz instructs his men to leave extra on the ground for her to pick up. This is in addition to Ruth's bold request to be closer to the front which we read just a few verses earlier.

Ruth finishes her day on the threshing floor, and verse 17 tells us that after her day's gleaning she ended up with an *ephah*. Most of us don't measure things in *ephahs* anymore; so, let me explain why that amount is such a big deal.

Ruth was supposed to be at the very back picking up the scraps with the other people who were just trying to get by. Most sources tell us that a person who spent their whole day gleaning like that could expect to collect between 1-2 pounds of grain. In comparison, an ephah was the equivalent of multiple gallons or about 29 pounds.[x]

Boaz's kindness allowed Ruth to gather in one day what it took most people to gather in an entire month! Ruth's bravery was rewarded with abundant provision.

God's provision for Ruth through Boaz may not be a "rule" for how He always works, but it is certainly not an exception. God regularly rewards our boldness with his provision.

In Luke 12, Jesus encourages his disciples to go out, spread the gospel, and to not let fear keep them back. He promises them, "Do not worry about what you will say, for the Holy Spirit will teach you at that time what you should say." In Matthew 14:29, Jesus calls Peter to step out of the boat and to walk towards him *on top of the water*. In Genesis 12:1, God calls Abram to leave his homeland but without even telling him his destination!

God constantly asks us to step out, to trust, and then to watch Him show up. Ruth had no idea what to expect when she left the house that morning.

We don't even know if she was trusting God for the outcome. All she knew was that she had a responsibility and waiting around for a miracle was not going to put food on the table.

Ruth took a step in the direction towards God's provision, and He showed up in a big way. Little did she know that a basket of food was only the beginning of what He had planned.

Takeaway: God rewards our bold action with His provision.

Prayer: Jehovah-jireh, God will provide. I believe this Father, please help me live out this truth.

David Ramos

Reviving Faith

Day 10
Ruth 2:18-23

Ruth enters the place Naomi and she are living with an incredible amount of food. Not only gleanings, but also fresh food from Boaz's table.

Naomi shoots off a flurry of questions; she's surprised, and for good reason. This kind of generosity doesn't usually happen, especially to a foreigner. Ruth answers her matter-of-factly: the man who helped me is named Boaz.

This is when the conversation changes course. We could almost imagine Naomi's eyes lighting up and the wheels in her head beginning to turn. She tells Ruth that he is a kinsman (or guardian) redeemer. At this point, we have no idea what that means and neither does Ruth. All we know is that he has been kind to her and, hopefully, this kindness will continue so that Ruth and Naomi can get back on their feet.

This section is another example of how important language is in the book of Ruth. To us, this is only a chance encounter which has led to God's provision. But Naomi is starting to see it as much more. Her language echoes other "betrothal-type scenes" in Scripture.[xi] Furthermore, she urges her daughter-in-law to stay with Boaz, to work with the women, and indirectly tells her to stay away from the other male workers. As we will learn, Naomi sees Boaz as an answer to the prayers she has been too angry to pray.

How do you revive a person's faith?

Hebrews 11:1 tells us, "Now faith is confidence in what we hope for and assurance about what we do not see." There's a few parts in here that I want to pull out which will help us understand what is happening to Naomi.

Faith consists of a confidence, or a belief, that some hope we have is possible and will come true. There has to be an object or an outcome we want in order for there to be hope. And we have to be courageous enough to believe in the hope in order for us to have faith.

Up until now, Naomi had no expected outcome. She believed the only reason she had returned home was to die and to leave Ruth alone to eventually die as well. But then Boaz entered the picture. Naomi saw no way out until God brought this unexpected character into their lives. The presence of Boaz produced an outcome she could hope for: Ruth getting married, having children, and saving the family line. However, what is really powerful here is not just that Naomi found something to hope in once again, but the fact that she *allowed* herself to hope again.

Ruth's courage came in the form of leaving her homeland and boldly facing the challenges in front of her. Naomi's courage is much more subtle but no less remarkable. Naomi dared to have faith once again after extreme loss.

Naomi allows herself to believe that life could be good once again, that her and Ruth's story is not over, and that maybe the God of Heaven and Earth does care.

The answer to how we revive faith is simple: we give ourselves or others a reason to hope again. Without hope there cannot be faith. And without faith, we will always fall short of the glorious lives God has planned for us.

Takeaway: Faith requires hope.

Prayer: Father, open my eyes to see that You have given me a reason to hope today.

God's Will Versus My Actions

Day 11
Ruth 3:1-5

Naomi's revived faith begins to free her from bitterness and stirs her to create a plan.

Boaz could be the one to give Ruth the life she deserves. So far, he has proven to be a man of character and someone who could look beyond Ruth's foreign status and see her for the woman she truly is.

The plan is simple, but risky. Naomi tells Ruth to sneak down to where Boaz will be tonight, wait until he is asleep, uncover his feet, and wait for what happens next.

Many scholars and commentators have worked to explain why Naomi suggested this particular plan for Ruth; but, in reality, it's just as strange as it sounds![xii] We can guess that Naomi wanted to protect both Ruth's and Boaz's reputations. So, by performing the "proposal" at night, if it went poorly, then no one else would have to know. As for uncovering the feet, while there are sexual overtones and suggestive language throughout Naomi's plan, it's likely that this would have been a gentle way of waking Boaz up since the cold night air would have bothered his feet enough to wake him.

We can imagine how strange the plan must have sounded to Ruth; but if it scared her, we wouldn't know, because she agrees to do it immediately. She trusts Naomi; and, perhaps, she is a little proud to see her boldness rubbing off on her mother-in-law.

Before we get too caught up in the excitement of what will follow, we have to ask a very important question. Was Naomi right to take the situation into her own hands? When is it okay for us to take bold action, and when will the bold action collide with what God already has planned?

I don't believe we get a black and white answer to that question in this text (or from any other passage in the Bible). But what we can do is pull out some guidelines to follow.

First, Naomi saw Ruth's and Boaz's run-in as a God-given opportunity and worked to make the most of it. There is something to be said about being an observant person. There really are no coincidences. If we have been praying for something, and suddenly a related opportunity comes across our paths – maybe that is God's way of saying, *"Hey this is for you!"*

Second, Naomi's motivation was love. Everything we do has a reason behind it, and often our motivations aren't as pure as we would like to believe they might be (at least I know mine aren't). The next time you are thinking about taking a bold action, especially one you feel God might be leading you towards, take the time to really search out the *why* behind it all.

Third, Naomi's boldness didn't cause Ruth to break any rules. Although her method was unorthodox, it was not immoral. Don't trick yourself into thinking that courageousness is a license to sin, however small. The outcome never justifies the means. It's the means which gives meaning to the outcome.

Don't be afraid to be bold for God, but never forget that He is working too.

Takeaway: We will not act against God's will so long as we remain observant, motivated by love, and keep the means God-glorifying.

Prayer: You know, Lord, that I can be stubborn at times. Guide me to act wisely when needed, and to wait patiently when required.

Selfless Example

Day 12

Ruth 3:6-11

Ruth wastes no time and follows Naomi's instructions immediately.

She makes her way down to the threshing floor, watches as Boaz falls asleep, then uncovers his feet and waits – all exactly as Naomi said. A short description might help paint a picture of what the scene would have looked like. Boaz's bed sat behind a very large pile of grain for privacy, and Ruth likely laid on the bed perpendicular to Boaz (like a "T"). The threshing area was built so that the wind could come in and help separate the parts of grain; so, there would have been many windows or open spaces for a draft. Once Boaz's feet were exposed, it probably didn't take long for him to wake up.

When Boaz did wake up, he was startled by some stranger laying at his feet. He calls out to discover who it is, and Ruth answers confidently: *"I am your servant, Ruth."*

I keep going back to the language, because so much is happening underneath the actual action of the scenes. This interaction between them is entirely different than their first meeting. Boaz no longer seeks out who she belongs to but asks into the darkness *what person is there*. Ruth responds not as a foreigner, or as someone who is less valuable, but replies as a full person, not just a "servant," as the text might suggest, but as a woman who is eligible for marriage, respectable, and a treasure to everyone God has put in her life.[xiii]

Ruth asks Boaz to cover her under the corner of his garment, an indirect way of asking for him to marry her, as well as an echo of *Ruth 2:12* where Boaz says God has covered her under his wing. To this opportunity, Boaz is overjoyed. He says her actions are even kinder than the ones which brought her all the way to Bethlehem with Naomi. Ruth could have done anything. She was a young woman in a foreign land with her whole life ahead of her. She could have chosen another young man and started a life, or an older rich man and fulfilled any of her earthly cravings. But she didn't do any of that. Instead, she chose to fulfill her commitment to her deceased husband and aging mother-in-law by pursuing a man who could continue their family line. Hubbard puts it like this, "She could have married for love or money, but she chose family loyalty instead."[xiv]

In everything, Ruth has constantly put herself last. Her wants, her needs – they have all taken a backseat to her duty as a daughter and a widow. Now, more than ever, she has put her fate in the hands of another and trusted that it would all work out.

Ruth teaches us that it is possible to be bold, yet selfless, courageous, yet humble. Ruth exemplifies faith in action, because everything she did was based on hope. Not on greed, or fear, or pride – like so many of our decisions are – but purely on the raw hope that God had a better plan for her life than she did. That she could end up anywhere and still be okay because of the One who was guiding her story.

Takeaway: It's possible to be bold for what you believe and remain selfless towards what you want.

Prayer: Thank You God for examples like Ruth, who show us what it means to live one's life for others.

Choosing Character

Day 13
Ruth 3:12-15

The moment the audience has been waiting for has finally arrived. Ruth and Boaz have laid their intentions and hopes entirely out in the open. Before we can celebrate, there is one more challenge they must overcome.

Boaz breaks the news that there is "another who is more closely related." This mysterious character seems to have come out of nowhere, and we are led to ask a number of questions. Why didn't this closer relative fulfill his duty? Did Naomi know about him? Will Ruth be unable to marry Boaz even after everything she has gone through?

The text leaves us with our curiosity and continues along. Ruth stays with Boaz until morning. He keeps her there for at least two reasons: to protect her from dangerous people who may be out at night, and to protect her reputation in case someone was to see her. Like Naomi's earlier directions, there is no sexual language present in Boaz's speech. Even in the dead of night when he is all alone with a beautiful young woman, he remains honorable.

As a final gesture of goodwill, Boaz sends Ruth home with a large bundle of barley. He then immediately heads into town to deal with the matter.

How can you know the path you are on is God's will?

Over my lifetime I have heard many conflicting arguments. *If life is too easy, you're definitely not in God's will. If life is too difficult, maybe that is God telling you to take a different path.* The advice goes both ways and can be incredibly frustrating when all you want to do is honor God with your choices.

From my study of the lives of these great Biblical characters, I believe a pattern begins to emerge. We can't measure whether or not we are in God's will by the ease or difficulty of our current circumstances. Those will change all the time. A much better guide is to ask the question:

"Am I living according to the character God has

called me to show?" Or put another way, "Am I *becoming the person God has called me to be?"*

In Scripture, becoming and doing always go hand in hand. The great men and women of God only accomplish great feats for His glory as they develop into persons of extraordinary character.

Ruth and Boaz are excellent examples of this. They had no idea what would happen at this point, but what they did know is that if they were faithful people of character – God would take care of the rest.

Figuring out what God wants you to do with your life is simple. Just focus on becoming the person He has called you to be.

Takeaway: God is more concerned with who we are becoming than what we are accomplishing.

Prayer: Heavenly Father, help me prioritize in my life what You believe is important; not what the world tells me to pursue.

David Ramos

Reason To Hope

Day 14

Ruth 3:16-18

Ruth arrives back home to Naomi early in the morning with a heaping bundle of barley. Naomi must be incredibly excited, as well as nervous. If last night's meeting went well, it could change the rest of her and her daughter-in-law's lives.

Ruth, who we imagine is just as ecstatic as her mother-in-law, retells everything that happened with Boaz. She probably explains the scene in detail: Boaz's honor, and the possible wrench in their plan. She ends her explanation by drawing attention back to the pile of food she has brought home.

Naomi is happy but uneasy. It's likely that she knew who the "closer relative" was before Boaz's revelation. Is there a reason she didn't approach him first? Perhaps resigning Ruth and herself to the status of poor widows was a better outcome then being redeemed by an unkind man. At this point, we don't know. All we can do is hope.

But there is good reason to hope. Ruth's choice of language in verse 17 echoes the ending of Chapter 1. When Naomi first enters the city, she tells people to call her Mara because she has returned empty. The phrasing of 3:17 prompts us to remember this scene, because in simplest terms it says, *"You will not return empty."* It forms a sort of bookend for the theme of Naomi's emptiness.[xv] Yes, she came into the city empty – but she came during the harvest season, and now this harvest will cause her to be filled again in every way.

God speaks through the simplest things. For Naomi, it was a pile of barley. For the disciple Peter (John 21), it was a net full of fish. God wants our attention. He wants us to know that He is aware of our needs, and wants, and fears; that He is active, powerful. And above all, that He not only knows, but He cares.

Like Naomi, deep pain can cause us to forget about God's goodness. It can harden us to His everyday miracles and keep us stuck. But it doesn't have to. Hope is what enables our eyes to see His goodness once again.

As we move into the last chapter of Ruth, all we have to hold onto is hope. Yet, hope is all God needs to break into our lives and fill us once again.

Takeaway: Don't let pain make you forget what hope led you to believe.

Prayer: Dear God, I believe that all things work together according to Your plan. Help me to remember that even when everything around me tells me otherwise.

David Ramos

A Nameless Legacy

Day 15

Ruth 4:1-8

Boaz wastes no time on his mission to redeem Naomi and Ruth. Once at the town gate, he begins to pull in all the necessary parts for his plan. First, the guardian-redeemer he needs to speak with is one of the first people to walk by. Perhaps this is a sign of God's grace over the situation. Second, Boaz calls together ten elders. It's likely there were many more than ten elders in the city, but that this particular case (the redemption of a relative's property) only required ten to be present.

Once everyone is gathered, Boaz jumps right into his speech. He explains Naomi's situation to the nameless kinsman-redeemer, focusing upon the sale of Naomi's land. At first, the man seems to go for it. However, this was all a part of Boaz's plan.

Only after the man has agreed to buy Naomi's land does Boaz bring up the subject of Ruth. Because they are widows, Naomi and Ruth come with the land. More than that, it would be the kinsman-redeemer's responsibility to give Ruth children so that Elimelek's family line would continue.

This twist has the exact effect Boaz was hoping for! The man backs off the deal and proclaims, *"Boaz, buy it yourself."*

Two questions stick in my mind after reading this passage of text. First, why did the prospect of marrying Ruth sound so unappealing to the kinsman-redeemer? Second, why would the writer of Ruth choose to keep the kinsman-redeemer, who is such an important character, nameless?

The commentator, Robert Hubbard, can help us answer the first question. If the kinsman-redeemer was only responsible for the land, he would have essentially grown his wealth through the transaction. That land would have become a part of his family's inheritance and been passed down to his children and so on. The prospect of adding a new wife to the mix changed all that. While he still would have gained the land, he would have had to bear more heirs with Ruth. Therefore, his own children wouldn't benefit at all from the transaction; or even worse, they could end up losing out since more of their family's resources and inheritance would have gone towards Ruth and the family they made together. He chose to protect what his family had, even at the cost of not fulfilling one of his familial duties.

This reason, I believe, also helps us answer the second question. As we have seen multiple times already in the book of Ruth, language plays a vital role. It not only communicates the story, but colors it powerfully. Here, the writer made a choice to leave this individual nameless.[xvi] Was it to protect his legacy? Or maybe the author wanted to keep the story as simple as possible? While we cannot know for sure, I believe the author was making a statement.

Because the kinsman-redeemer refused to fulfill his duties, and chose instead to worry about his own personal legacy, history has forgotten him.

When we choose to be selfish and look after ourselves at the expense of those closest to us, we also run the risk of living a forgettable life. All of us want our lives to mean something. Everyone hopes that the work, sweat, and tears they invested over a lifetime will last far beyond their own lives so that, in some way, a small part of them can also survive. It is possible, just not through the ways we usually go about it.

The only way to truly protect our lives and our legacies is to give them away. Ruth gave over her hopes, and dreams, and plans so that she could be loyal to Naomi. As we will see, Boaz put his own fortune and family line at risk so that he could show love towards Ruth. Both of these characters essentially gave their lives away, and in doing so, secured a legacy greater than they could have ever imagined.

Self-sacrifice is the way, my way, to finding yourself, your true self. Matthew 16:25 (MSG)

Takeaway: The only way to secure our legacies is to release them out of our hands and into God's.

Prayer: Thank You Lord for giving me this life, and for being the source of any legacy I could imagine.

Seeds Of Greatness

Day 16

Ruth 4:9-12

Boaz's plan has worked. His offer to fulfill the duties of a kinsman-redeemer have been accepted, and his new life with Ruth is about to begin.

The majority of these few verses are concerned with legal wording. Boaz is precise in his language. He will inherit the property of Naomi's husband and sons, as well as the foreign widow, Ruth. By doing this, Boaz will ensure the survival of his relative's family in addition to protecting their future standing within the city. Through a powerful act of love and boldness, Boaz has both helped to redeem past tragedies as well as secure future hopes.

The elders respond confidently and offer three comparisons in their speech. First, Ruth is compared to Rachel and Leah, the founding mothers of Israel. As a quick reminder, Jacob, who was later called Israel, married both Rachel and Leah. Their marriage was anything but perfect, and caused their entire family much grief. Yet in the end, the children of Rachel and Leah became the foundation of God's chosen nation. From them came the 12 tribes, and every clan within them. Comparing Ruth to Rachel and Leah was powerful, humbling, and meant that they fully accepted her as one of their own.

The second comparison is Boaz to Perez (*may your family be like that of Perez*). Perez was a twin (to Zerah) and the child of Judah (one of 12 sons of Rachel and Leah). Perez was supposed to be the second of the two twins, but during birth he broke out first and claimed his position as first born.[xvii] His struggle for preeminence continued as he grew, and the tribe of Perez became one of the most important clans in Israel. By comparing Boaz to Perez, they were not only hoping that Boaz would prosper from his generosity, but that his family line would swell into a guiding force within Israel.

The third, and final comparison, is between Ruth and Tamar at the very end of verse 12. While this comparison seems indirect, we only need to dig into Tamar's story a little to notice how many similarities there are to Ruth. Tamar's story takes place in Genesis 38. She was married to another one of Judah's sons, but he died before they could have children. It was Tamar's duty, like Ruth, to preserve her husband's line, but through a series of unfortunate events (and bad choices by men) Tamar was left childless and abandoned. But she wasn't about to accept her fate lying down. In a boldness that clearly echoes that of Ruth, she tricked her father-in-law, Judah, into sleeping with her and giving her children.

Tamar was a foreigner, just like Ruth, who was tasked to continue her husband's line and took bold measures to do so. While her methods were certainly less socially acceptable then Ruth's, her efforts led to birthing Perez (from above) who became one of the strongest clans in Israel.

All this is to say, the people of Bethlehem have great expectations for Boaz and Ruth. They have seen their character, their patience, their hope, and their faith in God and have concluded that if God does bless them with children – those little ones will certainly grow up to shape Israel's future.

The seeds of greatness are grown in the soil of struggle.

The people of Bethlehem saw everything Boaz and

Ruth had gone through to get to this point, and their reaction was to compare them to the great men and women who had come before them. Not to belittle their struggles, but to encourage them that all of their pain had been worth it. That, somehow, God was going to take their circumstances and glorify himself through them all. Nothing is wasted when given to God: no pains, no struggles, no delays. They are pieces of the puzzle He is building with our lives. And we are better for it.

Now we will see if Ruth's fate was as extraordinary as everyone hoped.

Takeaway: God can and will use every part of our story for His glory.

Prayer: I trust You Father, and I believe that every scrape and scar I have collected on my journey will play a part in the story You are writing with me.

Unanswered Questions

Day 17
Ruth 4:13-17a

As we enter the final paragraphs of Ruth, we can feel the joy and relief of the characters' situations. Ruth and Naomi have been through so much, but God has not let their cries go unanswered.

Much of this book echoes the lessons we find in the book of Job. In Job, we see an innocent man suffer for no apparent reason, but we end with a powerful conclusion – that although we will not understand much of what God does, we can trust in two things: God is always in control, and He is deeply good.

In these few verses we learn that Boaz and Ruth have indeed had a child, a son. We must remember how extraordinary this event truly is. Ruth was married to Naomi's son for 10 years without ever having a child! Now, God has opened her womb and provided a son. What follows next is equally as extraordinary.

The whole point of pairing up Ruth and Boaz was to fulfill the kinsman-redeemer duties and provide Elimelek's line with an heir. Ruth and Boaz have done that. But if you read the text closely, the story does not end with Ruth caring for her son. Verses 16 and 17a say that Naomi cared for the boy, and that the women of the town chanted, *"Naomi has a son."* So, what am I getting at?

It's likely that as a final act of kindness towards her mother-in-law, Ruth gave Naomi her firstborn son. Commentators agree that while the text does not reveal if Naomi became her legal mother or not, it suggests that she would be the one raising the child – not simply as a live-in grandmother, but as the one the child would grow up to see as his primary caregiver.

Ruth kept her promise to such a degree that she was willing to give her child away. At best, Naomi was hoping to be a part of her grandson's life, but God saw fit to give her even more.

If you are left with questions because of this scene, good. I don't think we are meant to know everything: why Ruth chose her actions, why Naomi ended up with another son, or why God guided these characters in this way. I believe the ending of Ruth is meant to leave us speechless. And that, like Naomi, seeing God work in such a way would lead us to become "believers who surrender to unanswered, bitter questions," and "embrace the certainty of God's blessed presence."[xviii]

This is the key to Ruth's extraordinary journey: boldness requires surrender. Ruth surrendered her fate to Naomi's God and found fulfillment. Boaz surrendered to his duty and was given a family. Naomi surrendered to hope and was restored a son.

Living an extraordinary story for God will always require extraordinary surrender. For it is in weakness that He gives us strength.[xix]

Takeaway: Taking bold action for God requires us to surrender the outcomes to Him.

Prayer: Almighty God, I want to do great things for You and with the life You have given me. Strengthen my spirit; all of me belongs to You.

Dare To Hope

Day 18
Ruth 4:17b-22

The name of Ruth's (and now Naomi's) son is Obed. For the important part language plays in the book of Ruth, it's strange that we aren't given any real clues as to what his name might mean. However, maybe this is on purpose since the story does not stop with Obed but continues. The narrator wants us to see one more thing: who eventually came from Obed.

Obed fathered Jesse, and Jesse fathered none other than the greatest ancient Israelite king, David.

The book of Ruth ends with a final, abbreviated genealogy. The genealogy begins with Perez, who was mentioned before, and continues down to Boaz. This was purposeful. We know we are missing a few names since there are more complete genealogies elsewhere in the Old

Testament (like 1 & 2 Chronicles). Scholars agree that the point of shortening the first two-thirds of the family line was to make Boaz appear *seventh* in line. This was a place of honor, and marked that history would remember him as a man of character.

After Boaz, the line resumes a standard pace. Obed was indeed the father of Jesse and the grandfather of king David. Which makes our Ruth the great-grandmother of king David.

If you take anything from the book of Ruth, I hope you will take this: God can use anyone, with any background, to accomplish anything, anywhere.

Don't let your familiarity with the story of Ruth cloud you from the greatness of this story! Things like this don't happen every day, but they can. God is at work every day. He is moving, and calling, and transforming circumstances right before our eyes. All we have to do is ask boldly to be a part of what He is doing.

God wants your life to become a beacon of His extraordinary grace – just like Ruth and Naomi's. He is looking to fulfill, bless, and restore in ways you cannot even imagine. And it all starts with hope.

Hope that God is who He says He is, so that we can surrender to His plan, and move boldly towards the opportunities He gives us.

So let us dare, like Ruth, and watch our God, who knows no limits, show up once again.

Takeaway: When we dare to hope in God, God defies the world with our lives.

Prayer: I am ready to hope in You Lord. Make me bold!

David Ramos

Continuing the Journey

Thank you for reading *Daring with Ruth*. I hope the experience was encouraging and that you've learned just a little bit more about one of the boldest characters in the Old Testament.

Now that you've started to learn some Old Testament truths, here are two steps you can take to continue your journey.

First, sign up for my newsletter at RamosAuthor.com. There you'll receive a monthly email that contains exclusive insights, book discounts, and the free gift *Dreaming with Joseph*.

Second, please take a minute to write a short review for *Daring with Ruth* on Amazon. These reviews help me write better, more effective books so I would deeply appreciate your support!

The one lesson from Ruth's story that I will never forget is this: a Christian is never beyond hope. Ruth and Naomi's situation seemed hopeless from the start, but that never stopped Ruth from boldly moving forward. She surrendered to God, then moved forward at a furious pace, believing that He would either guide her path or pick her up once she fell. How I wish we could be so bold!

I hope you will take the challenge and live a life characterized by surrender to God. It will be difficult, but that is why only the daring are remembered.

About the Author

David Ramos is an author and teacher passionate about communicating the life-changing truths found in the Old Testament. He has a degree in Classical and Medieval Studies and is currently finishing a Master's in Religion (Biblical Studies) at Ashland Theological Seminary. When he's not writing you can usually find David chasing down the newest food truck or helping his fiancé Breahna plan their wedding (2016).

David and his library currently reside in Cleveland, Ohio.

Visit his website at ramosauthor.com or on Facebook.com/DavidRamosAuthor.

More Books by David Ramos

The Bible Habit: 7 Strategies on How to Study the Bible

Crowned with David: 40 Devotionals to Inspire Your Life, Fuel Your Trust, and Help You Succeed in God's Way

Enduring with Job: 30 Devotionals to Give You Hope, Stir Your Faith, and Find God's Power in Your Pain

Climbing with Abraham: 30 Devotionals to Help You Grow Your Faith, Build Your Life, and Discover God's Calling

Escaping with Jacob: 30 Devotionals to Help You Find Your Identity, Forgive Your Past, and Walk in Your Purpose

The God with a Plan

The Shadow of Gethsemane: An Easter Poem

Further Reading on Ruth

The Message of Ruth: The Wings of Refuge by David J. Atkinson

Faithful God by Sinclair Ferguson

Ruth: Under the Wings of God by John Piper

The Gospel of Ruth: Loving God Enough to Break the Rules by Carolyn Custis James

Takeaway List

1. Sometimes life's detours are God's shortcuts.
2. Painful periods in life are opportunities to trust in God's pattern of provision.
3. It's possible to be angry at God and still trust in Him.
4. Never underestimate what God can do with a willing soul.
5. Life is a series of seasons. Your current trouble will eventually bloom into something good.
6. God still works miracles today.
7. Deep prayers and courageous actions invite God's incredible goodness into our lives.
8. God cares more than you could fathom and is closer than you think.
9. God rewards our bold action with His provision.
10. Faith requires hope.
11. We will not act against God's will so long as we remain observant, motivated by love, and keep the means God-glorifying.
12. It's possible to be bold for what you believe and remain selfless towards what you want.

13. God is more concerned with who we are becoming than what we are accomplishing.

14. Don't let pain make you forget what hope led you to believe.

15. The only way to secure our legacies is to release them out of our hands and into God's.

16. God can and will use every part of our story for His glory.

17. Taking bold action for God requires us to surrender the outcomes to Him.

18. When we dare to hope in God, God defies the world with our lives.

[i] Robert L. Hubbard Jr., *The Book of Ruth* from *The New International Commentary on the Old Testament* (Grand Rapids: William B. Eerdmans Publishing Company, 1988), 85.
[ii] Hubbard Jr., 97.
[iii] Hebrews 13:8
[iv] Psalm 77
[v] Hubbard Jr., 103.
[vi] Ibid., 113.
[vii] Ibid., 115.
[viii] Ibid., 133.
[ix] 2 Timothy 1:7
[x] Hubbard Jr., 179.
[xi] Ibid., 187.
[xii] Ibid., 204.
[xiii] Ibid., 211.
[xiv] Ibid., 214.
[xv] Ibid., 225.
[xvi] Ibid., 234.
[xvii] Genesis 38:27-30
[xviii] Hubbard Jr., 275.
[xix] 2 Corinthians 12:9-10

Made in the USA
Monee, IL
17 September 2024

66029388R00053